From Little Seeds to Great Fortunes:
The Magic of Long Term Investing!

Book 5 of the My First Finance Coloring Book Series

Written by: Ben Hofstetter and Nick Zehrung

TABLE OF CONTENTS

Part 1:

From Little Seeds to Great Fortunes: the Power of Long Term Investing!

For Parents

Key Themes Explored in this chapter:

- In this chapter, we dive into the importance of long-term investing and how it plays a crucial role in building future wealth. We illustrate this concept by taking a close look at a small apple seed, which represents an initial investment. Over time, we witness the transformation of this seed into a magnificent orchard, just like an investment portfolio would grow over time.
- We explore the concept of compound interest by observing the growth of the first apple tree as it matures and starts producing its own apples. These apples, in turn, have the potential to become new apple trees. This process showcases the power of compound interest, which exhibits an exponential yield curve over time.
- Activity to Try at Home!: Engage your child in a fun experiment to demonstrate the concept of compound interest and its exponential growth. Offer them a small piece of candy today and present them with the choice to wait a week to receive two pieces of candy instead. If they choose to wait then give them the choice to take two pieces of candy the next week or offer them the option to wait another week for four pieces of candy. Repeat this activity to illustrate how patience and delayed gratification can lead to significant rewards over time, just like the power of compound interest. This hands-on experience will help them understand the concept in a real-life context.

In the books we've read, we learned many important things. Book 1 showed us how we make money by helping others. Book 2 taught us about saving and budgeting. Book 3 focused on investing, and Book 4 taught us about helping our community. Do you know what's cool about all these things? The more time we give them, the better they become, just like growing a giant tree!

Imagine if making money were as magical as planting a tiny apple seed and watching it grow into a magnificent orchard over time!

Just like starting with a small apple to grow an apple tree, we began our money-growing adventure by saving our spare change in the magical piggy bank we learned about in Book 2!

Just like an apple tree needs water to grow into a big, strong tree, our investments need money to grow too! Think of the money we add to our investments like it's the water we give the tree.

We'll learn more about this exciting idea on the next page of our adventure!

You have two options when it comes to watering your tree. You can use a watering can and do it yourself every day, or you can set up a special sprinkler system that does it automatically!

Just like the sprinkler system takes care of watering the tree without you needing to think about it, setting up your investments to happen automatically is the best way to let them grow over time!

As we keep watering our apple tree, something magical happens. It grows bigger and stronger, and before we know it, it starts to produce its very own apples! This is when the real excitement of growing an apple orchard, and investing, begins!

Guess what? Our apple tree has a surprise for us! The apples it produces can be used to plant and grow new trees! Isn't that amazing?

Just like the apples creating new trees, your investments have the power to grow money for themselves over time! It's like a magical cycle of growth and prosperity!

Amazing news! Our one little apple has had enough time to grow and become a magnificent orchard! Isn't that incredible?

In the grown-up world, this is like Compound Interest, but for now, let's remember that investing over time is the secret to making money! It's like a magical recipe for growing your wealth and reaching your dreams!

Remember when we invested in lemonade stands with our class in Book 3? Back then, we asked for our money back right away from our teacher. But what if we decided to let them keep our money a little longer? Let's explore what magical things can happen when we give our money more time to grow!

Time is like a superpower when it comes to making money, just like we saw with the apple orchard!

In the class example, there were two lemonade stands that lost money because of a rainstorm. We decided to take our money out of the mutual fund by asking our teacher for it back. But you know what? If we had waited just one more week, those two lemonade stands would have made even more money when the sun came out!

This teaches us an important lesson: being patient with our money and investments can lead to even more money in the end!

In the exciting world of investing, there's a valuable lesson to remember: small actions over time can lead to your money growing more! It's like when we watered the tiny apple every single day. Before we knew it, that little seed grew into a magnificent orchard filled with delicious apples!

Part 2:

Money is Time: Using Money to Chase our Dreams!

For Parents

Key Themes Explored in this chapter:

- In this chapter, we conclude the entire series by introducing a fresh perspective on money: money equals time. We delve into this idea by examining the process of buying an apple from the store instead of growing an apple tree from a seed. By purchasing the apple, we are essentially acquiring not just the fruit itself, but also the months of effort and labor that would have been required to grow the tree and produce the apple.

- We delve into the profound impact of this simple mental shift - from using money to purchase things, to using money to buy time - and how it can grant us the freedom to pursue any dream we envision in the future. By recognizing that money is just a tool to create more time for ourselves, we open up a world of possibilities and empower ourselves to chase our dreams with a strong financial backing.

- We conclude the series with a message of hope and appreciation for the invaluable gift you, as parents, are providing to your children. By teaching them financial literacy from a young age, you are equipping them with the tools and knowledge to accomplish their goals and navigate their financial future with confidence. Your dedication to their financial education is an investment that will yield lifelong benefits and set them on a path towards financial independence and success.

In the first book of this series, we learned that money can be used to buy the things we want or need. But as you've explored these books, have you ever wondered if there's a different way to think about money?

Well, here's an exciting idea: What if we think of money as time!?

Here's a fun way to understand it! Imagine you're at the store with your parents, and you spot a yummy apple you want to snack on. When you buy that apple, you're not only getting the fruit, but also the time it would have taken to grow it yourself!

Instead of waiting a long time to grow your own apple, you can pay someone else to do it for you. That way, you can enjoy the apple without all the waiting!

Now, here's where things get interesting! When we think of money as time, it changes how we do things in life, and it's pretty cool!

We start seeing money as a tool that helps us create a future where we can spend our time doing what we love instead of doing things just to make money.

Think of it like this: the more money we have, the more fun things we can do! That's why it's important to learn about money when we're young.

Remember the apple trees? Just like they grow and give us more apples over time, our investments can grow too! So if we start investing early, we'll make more money and have more time for fun activities later on!

Let's do a little more imagining!
Think about what you want to be when you grow up and draw the picture in the space above!

Maybe you want to be a real life superhero, like a firefighter, and help people all day?

Or maybe you want to spread joy by streaming all the newest video games and showing people all the fun ways to play?

Maybe you want to explore the final frontier by being an Astronaut and going to the Moon or Mars with NASA?

No matter what you decide to do when you grow up, you will be awesome at it!

But here's the last lesson: knowing about money can make your life even more enjoyable. When you understand how money works and how to manage it wisely, you won't have to worry about not having enough. That way, you can focus on doing what you love and being happy in your chosen career!

Hooray! You've finished the whole coloring book series and learned so much about money and time. That's amazing! Remember, the things you've learned will be with you forever. By being smart about your money and time, you can make your future really awesome. So keep on exploring, keep on learning, and make every moment count. Your future is full of possibilities, and you're ready to make it bright and successful!

For Parents

Afterword:

Nick and I embarked on the journey of creating the "My First Financial Literacy Book" series because we have witnessed firsthand the challenges faced by young adults in managing their finances and the overwhelming stress caused by a lack of financial literacy. As young Officers in the U.S. Army, we often found ourselves consoling fellow Soldiers who had lost all their money due to a lack of understanding about personal finances. On multiple occasions, we found ourselves confronting predatory payday lenders on behalf of our Soldiers. It was clear to us that if these 18-year-old individuals targeted by such lenders were financially literate, they would have been able to avoid the need for these types of loans. Even after transitioning into the civilian world, we continue to observe these same mistakes repeating themselves, with some taking over two decades to rectify.

It is our mission to empower future generations by equipping them with essential financial knowledge, and we sincerely appreciate your support on this Financial Literacy journey. Stay tuned for our upcoming series as we strive to make a positive impact on the financial well-being of as many children as possible.